ADORABLE

ZUCCHINI

(Courgettes)

MORE MAGIC THAN THE PUMPKIN

D0927128

ADORABLE
ZUCCHINI
(Courgettes)
MORE MAGIC THAN THE PUMPKIN

by Naomi Barry

Interior Illustrations
Jane Lawrence

Cover Illustration
Lisa Adams

The Brick Tower Press ®
1230 Park Avenue, New York, NY 10128
Copyright © 2005
by Naomi Barry

Barry, Naomi
The Traditional Country Life Recipe Series:
Includes Index
ISBN 1-883283-33-7, softcover

Library of Congress Catalog Card
Number: 2005920557
First Edition, June 2005

TABLE OF CONTENTS

Acknowledgements

A Great Thank You to Bettina McNulty and to Ardenio Alvaro.

Bettina–always spot on for a good idea - was the sparkplug for this book. One September in Porto Ercole on the Tuscan coast, the brilliant Candida was spoiling us daily with royal meals, yet keeping a respectful eye on the budget.

"Have you noticed how many of her marvelous dishes include Zucchini,"said Bettina. "I think Zucchini deserves a book on its own." She herself had a sheaf of recipes of this versatile vegetable and that was the start.

Later in my Paris kitchen, Ardenio cooked zucchini in a hundred possible ways. For months we ate zucchini. So great was the variety, we were never bored. Can one ask for higher praise?

So thanks for this.

INTRODUCTION

I have a passion for zucchini. I also have a passion for Blini with Black Caviar. For obvious reasons it can't be an Everyday Passion like zucchini which in comparison costs almost nothing at all.

You could never tell by the looking that this variety of summer squash, cucumber in shape but with a smooth glossy skin, has such a potential for reinventing itself that one could eat it 10 days in a row, never bored, always with pleasure.

When Life makes one of its entertaining demands, zucchini usually can rescue the situation. Friends casually drop in for a drink. The cupboard is bare of Nibbles. Within minutes a heap of deep-fried zucchini "Matchsticks" can be brought forth. Crisp, salted morsels, addictive as peanuts.

How does one produce a festive supper for six visiting relatives on a weekend that the budget couldn't be more battered? If ever there were a dish that could be subtitled "Soul of Hospitality," it is a melting Zucchini alla Parmigiana.

Zucchini is modesty itself. The "Virtues" sneak up on you. By then you have become a devotee. The list of attributes is impressive:

(a) The flavor is subtle and delicate. For Italians, the great connoisseurs of zucchini, the flavor is incomparable in early Spring when the eagerly awaited first specimens arrive, tender as butter or a baby's toes.

(b) There is the deuces-wild versatility which enables it to slip into every category–soups, salads, snacks, hors d'oeuvres, main courses, cakes. "You mean there's zucchini in this!" exclaim the uninitiated and take a second helping.

(c) Economy is a lure provided it doesn't show. I would never call zucchini my affordable passion if it were not capable of a few dishes stylish enough for a banquet buffet. Style at a bargain price is always irresistible.

(d) No waste. Zucchini is edible end to end, skin included. As a bonus, there are the big gorgeous yellow flowers. Stuffed and deep-fried or butterflied and fried, they are a gourmet's delight.

(e) The story of *Why Do I Love You* is better told in the recipes collected here. There is not a dud among them.

Zucchini is one of the 1000 members of the *Cucurbita* family of gourds. The extended family is so far flung that the back scrubbing loofah is a distant relative, a rather serendipity relationship. More familiar kissing cousins of zucchini are pumpkin, cucumber, musk melon, watermelon, and such squashes as scallop, summer crookshank, and pattypan. (See Bruce T. Paddock's introduction to *Pumpkin Companion* in this series, pp 3-4.)

Ancestors of the zucchini supposedly were native to Central America. From there they made their way to Europe in the 16th century. Apparently, however, the genus in one form or another existed throughout the ancient world, particularly around the Mediterranean. Since the Roman Empire embraced the entire

Mediterranean, it is not surprising that zucchini is a staple in the cuisines of the countries bordering that sea. Spicing changes with the region. North Africa favors cumin. Europe is partial to basil, thyme, and flat parsley.

According to the *Oxford Companion to Food* and its erudite editor Alan Davidson, "It seems clear that it was the Italians who first marketed vegetable marrows in a small size. It is therefore appropriate to choose their name Zucchini rather than the French name Courgettes. As Zucchini they had a late arrival in the U.S.A. where Italian immigrants made the introduction."

(Incidentally, the English use the French appellation, Courgettes. The difference can be confusing but it is only semantic.)

Zucchini range in color from ivory to dark green. Shades of green predominate. The shiny smoothness of the skin is the keynote. The shape varies from round to oblong with a rounded end. The round resemble green apples and are used mainly for stuffing. The presentation can be charming. The elongated ones adapt themselves to all modes and manner.

Zucchini usually are harvested in a young unripe stage. If they are not, they ought to be because for good eating zucchini should measure from four to six inches. At seven inches they are still possible. At eight inches I close my eyes and say, "Maybe for soup." Beyond eight inches...be firm. Don't buy!

The ideal is three-and-a-half to six inches. with size, flavor decreases, centers fill up with seeds and the flesh bloats with water. Whatever the length make certain the skin is shining and unblemished. Any brown at the ends is a sign of age.

I am outraged by the monstrous specimens I sometimes see on sale in markets. Unfit. How dare they?

Left on its own zucchini will continue to grow like Jack's Beanstalk. Phenomenal perhaps but not for eating.

My friend Ulrika learned the folly of letting nature run rampant. She went off on vacation without leaving instructions to curb her patch. When she returned, the ground was a nightmare of awesome zucchini looking like baseball bats or policemen's truncheons. Resourcefully she used them to weight down a tarpaulin that might otherwise have blown away. They served their new purpose admirably.

During their prime season, zucchini seem to spring up overnight. What wasn't there yesterday is ready for picking at dawn today. They grow with such abandon that on a dewy morning one might well scream, "Heaven's to Betsy, what am I supposed to do with them?"

"Pick them, my dear, at once. And enjoy them."

Elizabeth David, the celebrated British gastronomic writer, championed the cause of baby zucchini so forcefully that growers actually bowed to her wishes. Her influence was equally felt by the public.

In the *Oxford Companion to Food*, Alan Davidson wrote that zucchini "only became popular in England after Elizabeth David in the 1950s and 1960s had introduced them to readers of her books."

Grow Your Own was the dictum of Jane Grigson, another British cookbook writer. "Even if you haven't a garden, you can buy a couple of zucchini plants from a nurseryman and grow them in the backyard or on a balcony in a tub. Until you have grown them yourself and picked them at 2-5 inches in length you cannot imagine how delicious they can be. Put them straight into the pan with a knob of butter and seasoning. Jam on the lid with foil and stew gently for about five minutes. That is all you should do with so perfect and fresh a vegetable."

Recognizing that shop zucchini would be larger, she warned, "Reject them if the skin is so tough that it cannot be wrinkled easily with your fingernail; once it hardens, the zucchini is on the decline into vegetable marrow."

The wives of Mediterranean farmers and fishermen long ago discovered that a few zucchini in their kitchens were a bonanza. Adept at using whatever was at hand, these women began to experiment. The growing repertory was much appreciated but it remained local.

So local that in 1902 when Auguste Escoffier completed his voluminous *Guide Culinaire* for professional chefs, zucchini received only one entry, a recipe for à la Provençale, a gratin of rice pilaf and zucchini slices pre-cooked in butter and bound together with a béchamel sauce. To the ladies who lived in the shade of olive trees, this concoction would have seemed as alien as Cutlets Pojarsky.

Beneath the recipe a *nota* in minus-cule print stated "In Provence zucchini are prepared like eggplant–be it stuffed, fried, sautéed etc." The low billing was an authoritative brush-off.

Escoffier was Caesar Ritz's sidekick in all the grand hotels Ritz was opening throughout Europe. Although Escoffier was born in Provence, obviously he did not regard zucchini as up to the mark for the flossy clientele of Ritz's "Palace Hotels." On the other hand his *Guide Culinaire* gave 10 detailed recipes for eggplant.

Styles change. Tastes change. A Neapolitan gourmet told Elizabeth David that every dish containing eggplant would be far better if zucchini were used instead. We took the advice to heart. The results were lighter and more delicate. Try substituting zucchini in the classic Eggplant alla Parmigiana and you too will be convinced.

During the past 20 years the leading chefs have been reversing Escoffier's oversight, creating fanciful dishes with zucchini to serve in their stratospherically-priced establishments. International acceptance was on the way.

Jean-Louis Palladin (the French chef who bedazzled Washington D.C. during the 1990s) alternated slices of zucchini and Maine lobster to produce an elegant rosette set atop a golden sauce of smelt roe. In Paris, the legendary Joel Robuchon transformed zucchini into a refined mousse enhanced with filaments of saffron. The stylish first course presented three ovals of the mousse on a base of tomato coulis.

Now the chefs, the ones who set the styles world wide, have been turning their attention to zucchini flowers. This is a hitherto unexplored area for fantasy. One extravaganza had the flower filled with a farce consisting of a mousseline of lobster spiked with slivers of black truffle, a divertimento fit for Lucullus' table.

My more earth-bound introduction to zucchini was through Candida, the most talented cook in Porto Ercole, a fishing port on the coast of Tuscany where we have been lucky enough to have a toe-hold for some years. Candida is self-taught in the sense that she learned cooking from her mother who learned from her mother who learned from her mother in the famous "At-the-Elbow" system. In addition to generations of accumulated know-how, she has a touch of genius at the tip of her tongue.

Zucchini is part of Candida's daily menu for more than six months a year. Her motto might be "Every day perhaps but never quite the same." When you think you have exhausted her stock of recipes, another will tumble out her sleeve. We have included some of them here. Because her palate is so sure, they are foolproof.

I once met the daughter of Gulbenkian, called "Mr. Five-by-Five" because at the beginning of the 20th century he worked out deals with the pioneer oil companies who were to pay him 5% in perpetuity. "Anybody can be a great cook with caviar and foie gras," said the wise heiress, "what counts is to be amusing."

Mozzarella, capers, anchovy… these are Candida's ingredients to tuck into a zucchini flower . The batter is simply flour, water, salt. The components could not be more simple, the result more amusing.

If I may submit a candidate for "People's Choice for Gastronomic Heaven," I'd say "zucchini."

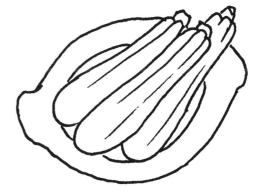

MATCHSTICKS

Note: These are as addictive as peanuts.

(1) Cut zucchini into matchsticks, 1/4-inch thick.
(2) Flour lightly. Shake off the excess flour.
(3) In a pot large enough to hold the cut zucchini, add the peanut oil and heat until just boiling.
(4) Throw the cut zucchini into the hot peanut oil and take care to avoid the hot splattering oil. As soon as golden brown, remove with a perforated skimmer.
(4) Drain on absorbent paper.
(5) Heap on a platter. Salt generously. The heap will disappear in a flash.

▣ INGREDIENTS

4 medium zucchini.
flour, enough to coat the zucchini lightly
salt to taste
4 cups of peanut oil for deep frying

NOTE: Matchsticks should be served hot. They are an agreeable accompaniment to drinks and wonderfully economic.

SERVES 4

FRITTERS

(1) Soften onion in butter.

(2) In a large bowl, mix well the onion, zucchini, eggs, cheese, parsley, mint, salt, pepper, and cayenne.

(3) Little by little, sift in the flour.

(4) Drop by spoonful into skillet and fry in heated oil. Press down with back of spoon so fritters will be slim.

(5) Brown on both sides. Drain on absorbent kitchen paper and serve.

NOTE: *We euphemistically named these fritters Silver Dollars because of their shape and because of the way people dive for them. Serve with drinks.*

▓ INGREDIENTS

1 small onion, finely chopped
1 tablespoon of butter
3 small zucchini, shredded and squeezed dry
2 eggs, lightly beaten with a fork
1/2 cup of fresh mint, scissored into ribbons
1/2 cup of flat parsley, chopped
1/2 cup of grated Gruyère cheese
1/2 cup of flour
salt, pepper, and cayenne pepper to taste
vegetable oil for frying but grape seed oil is particularly good

SERVES: APPROXIMATELY 30

FRITELLINI

(1) Shred zucchini and carrots. Chop onion fine. String celery and chop into small bits. Mix with parsley and beaten egg.

(2) Toss everything into the Tempura Batter which, if necessary, can be made several hours ahead and kept in the refrigerator until ready to use. Season with salt and pepper.

(3) Drop by small spoonful into hot oil. When golden on both sides, remove the fritellini and drain onto kitchen paper. Continue with the next batch.

NOTE: *Serve them hot. Rush out more. There rarely seem to be enough. Can be dipped into soy sauce or Worcestershire sauce or simply dusted with salt.*

NOTE: *Finger Food to go with drinks … hot and irresistible.*

▨ INGREDIENTS

2 small zucchini
2 small carrots
1 small onion
1 or 2 stalks of celery
salt and pepper to taste
1 egg
generous handful of chopped
    parsley

TEMPURA BATTER

1 small egg
1/2 cup of flour
1/4 cup of ice water
salt to taste

(1) Whisk together egg, flour, and 1/4 cup of ice water. Whisk until smooth. Slowly add remaining water and a pinch of salt. Stir until you achieve a batter like thick cream.

SERVES 4

MINIATURE MEAT BALLS
FOR A GREEK OR TURKISH STYLE "MEZES"

(1) Combine all the ingredients and shape into walnut-sized balls.
(2) Roll in flour and dust off the excess.
(3) Fry over low heat in a mixture of butter and olive oil. Spear with toothpicks and serve.

▨ INGREDIENTS

1/3 pound of ground beef
1/3 pound of ground pork
1/3 pound of ground veal
1 egg, beaten
salt and pepper to taste
grated zest of 1 lemon
1/2 cup of grated zucchini, squeezed dry
cracker crumbs or day-old bread, soaked in milk and squeezed dry (just enough to bind the mixture)

SERVES 6-8

SAVORY MINI CREPES

(1) Grate zucchini. Squeeze dry. Season with salt and pepper
(2) Add one beaten egg
(3) Slowly incorporate the flour sieved with baking powder.
(4) Drop by tablespoonful onto a hot griddle. Brown on both sides.
(5) Pour on melted butter. Sprinkle with Parmesan. Serve immediately.

▨ INGREDIENTS

1 1/2 pounds of zucchini
1/2 cup of flour
1 teaspoon of baking powder
1 egg
salt and pepper to taste
melted butter
grated Parmesan cheese

NOTE: Nice to serve in the living room before sitting down to dinner.

MAKES ABOUT
20 MINI-CREPES

SUMMER GOODNESS

(1) Serve well-chilled on the dinner table or passed around with drinks.

▩ INGREDIENTS

zucchini, cut into julienne sticks (tender, fresh, uncooked and healthy)

baby carrot sticks, cut into julienne sticks

celery hearts

fennel, sliced thinly

small radishes, root removed

cherry tomatoes

SERVES 4

ZUCCHINI MINI CUPS
WITH RED CAVIAR OR SMOKED SALMON

NOTE: An exquisite bite for a buffet or a cocktail party tray.

(1) Cut zucchini crosswise into 1-inch thick chunks. Scoop out the centers, leaving a 1/4-inch rim all around, to form little cups. Stand them upright in a shallow roasting pan.

(2) Place a dot of butter at the bottom of each zucchini cup. Spoon in the chicken consommé to fill each cup. Pour the remaining consommé into the roasting pan around the zucchini cups. Cover with aluminum foil.

(3) Bake in a pre-heated oven 15 minutes at 400° F.

(4) Drain off liquid from cups and from the roasting pan. Transfer to a saucepan and reduce to about 2 tablespoons. Paint the cups inside and out with this reduction. Set the cups aside to cool.

(5) Mix the sour cream or the crème fraîche with the snipped dill and spoon it halfway into each zucchini cup.

(6) Top with a small mound of red caviar or smoked salmon scissored into bits.

NOTE: Decorate with a sprig of dill or a blade of chives, planted upright.

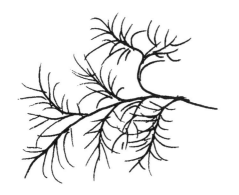

⬚ INGREDIENTS

5 zucchini, 4 to 6 inches long
1 1/2 cups of Consommé
butter
sour cream or crème fraîche
red caviar or smoked salmon
fresh dill

NOTE: *Part of the charm of these
frivolities is their Thumbelina size.
A cup no more than an inch high
can be popped whole into the
mouth without disturbing decorum.
Larger would be a mess. The delicious combination is worth the
effort to measure with precision.
Furthermore, a line-up of the little
green cups with their pink or red
toppings couldn't be prettier.*

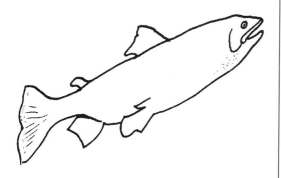

SERVES 3-4

ZUCCHINI FRITTERS

NOTE: Paul Bocuse likes to pair roast lamb with a heaping platter of zucchini fritters.

(1) In a bowl, combine flour, salt, melted butter, and beer.

(2) Pass through a sieve to remove any lumps. Chill for 1 1/2 hours in the refrigerator.

(3) Beat egg stiff, and fold into chilled batter.

(4) Dip the zucchini slices in the batter. Group in batches and fry in hot peanut oil or grapeseed oil. Drain. Keep warm in the oven with the door ajar until all the fritters are done. Serve at once.

⊞ INGREDIENTS

1 pound of zucchini, sliced crosswise into 1 1/4-inch slices, patted dry
peanut or grapeseed oil for frying

BATTER

3/4 cup of flour
salt
2 tablespoons of butter, melted
1 cup of beer
1 egg white, stiffly beaten

FRIED FLOWERS

Simple version,

(1) Open the flowers on one side
    without separating them from
    the base. Open flat, butterfly
    fashion.
(2) Dip into the Pastella batter, drip-
    ping off any excess.
(3) Slip into the hot oil. When gold-
    en brown on both sides, drain on
    kitchen paper.
(4) Sprinkle with salt, then serve
    while still hot.

▨ INGREDIENTS

zucchini flowers, 3 or 4 flowers for
   each person
Pastella batter (see below)
flour, water, and salt
vegetable or peanut oil, sufficient
   quantity for deep frying

Pastella (flour and water)
1 cup of flour
water
salt to taste

(1) Put sifted flour in a soup
    dish. Gradually add cold
    water, constantly beating
    with a fork. Add a pinch of
    salt. The pastella will be like
    cream.

NOTE: *This simple water and flour
    batter produces a lovely light
    crust.*

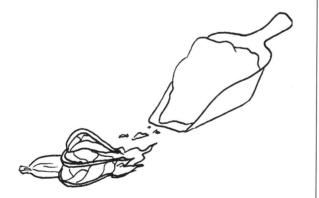

STUFFED FLOWERS OF ZUCCHINI

(1) Wash anchovy fillets under cold running water. Dry and cut into 3 or 4 pieces.

(2) Drain zucchini flowers, and pat dry. Carefully separate petals. Insert the following into the flower: small cubes of mozzarella, bits of anchovy, a few capers.

(3) Tuck in the petals. Dip each flower into the Pastella batter. Let any excess drip off.

(4) Deep fry in the peanut oil until golden. Remove with skimmer. Drain on absorbent paper.

▧ INGREDIENTS

zucchini flowers
mozzarella cheese
2 anchovy fillets
capers
Pastella batter (see page 19)
4 cups of vegetable or peanut oil, sufficient quantity for deep frying

NOTE: The gorgeous showy yellow blossoms are gathered in the early morning and kept fresh immersed in very cold water.

NOTE: Proof that a little bit of "almost nothing" can reach sublime.

Count on 4 or 5 flowers for each person. (There never seem to be enough.)

EGYPTIAN CROQUETTES

(1) Grate the zucchini.
(2) Place in a non-stick pan over medium heat. Cook until all the water evaporates. Stir constantly.
(3) Remove from heat. Allow to cool.
(4) Mix with beaten egg yolks. Add salt, pepper, and 1 tablespoon of flour.
(5) Heat the cumin briefly in a dry pan. Remove. Pound to a powder. Add to zucchini mixture.
(6) With floured hands, form croquettes. Flatten slightly with your palms. Roll in flour. Fry in hot vegetable oil. Drain on absorbent paper. Serve.

NOTE: *A Taste of Cairo.*

▩ INGREDIENTS

2 pounds of zucchini
2 egg yolks
salt and pepper to taste
flour
1/2 teaspoon of cumin seeds
vegetable or peanut oil for frying

NOTE: *Spear each croquette with a toothpick and dip into a mixture of 1 part Dijon Mustard with 3 parts Mayonnaise.*

Makes about 30 small croquettes.

A SOUP OF EMERALD GREEN

(1) In a large pot, gently fry the onion and curry powder in olive oil until onion is translucent and curry loses its raw taste.

(2) Add boiling water, bouillon cube, and zucchini.

(3) Simmer for 15 minutes. Add parsley. Cook about 3 minutes more. Pass through a vegetable mill or food processor. Correct seasoning. Reheat. Squeeze lemon.

(4) Top with croutons; a dollop of sour cream, thick yogurt or crème fraîche. Sprinkle the top with Parmesan cheese and serve.

▨ INGREDIENTS

1 large onion
1 teaspoon of curry powder
4 cups of water
1 chicken bouillon cube
1 pound of zucchini
generous dose of flat Italian parsley, coarsely chopped
salt and pepper to taste
squeeze of lemon juice
handful of croutons, sautéed in butter
2 tablespoons of heavy cream, crème fraîche or yogurt
Parmesan cheese, grated as a topping

NOTE: A white glove start for a dinner party and the bonus of minimum effort.

SERVES 4

AN ALSATIAN TART

(1) Slice the zucchini into 1/4-inch thick pieces. Sauté in butter until golden. Take care not to overcook.

(2) Sauté bacon. Drain well. Cut into 1-inch squares. If you have access to a thick slab of bacon, cut in cubes, blanch, and sauté the cubes lightly. Set aside.

(3) Mix the cream, beaten eggs, salt, pepper, nutmeg, and cayenne.

(4) Place the zucchini on the partially baked pie shell. Scatter top with the bacon bits.

(5) Pour on the cream and egg mixture. Sprinkle with grated cheeses.

(6) Bake in a preheated oven for 20 minutes at 375°F.

NOTE: *Cut into wedges and serve directly from the pie pan.*

▣ INGREDIENTS

2 pounds of zucchini
1 tablespoon of butter
6 strips of bacon or 1/4-pound slab of bacon
2 cups of light cream
4 eggs, beaten
salt and pepper to taste
pinch of nutmeg
pinch of cayenne
partially baked pie shell
2 ounces of grated cheese, a mixture of Parmesan and Gruyère

CREAM

SERVES 6-8

ONE-CRUST PASTRY
FOR ALSATIAN TART

(1) Using the dough attachment of a food processor, mix flour, sugar, salt, and softened butter. Add egg yolk and ice water. Mix well. Wrap the ball of dough in plastic wrap or a damp dish towel.

(2) Chill for at least half an hour.

(3) Roll out on floured board. Butter a 10-inch fluted pie pan. Pat the dough with your hands into the pan allowing for overlap to hang down the sides.

(4) Prick a few holes in dough with the tines of a fork. Place weights in the pan to keep the dough from rising during baking.

(5) Bake 10 minutes in a pre-heated 375°F. oven.

▨ INGREDIENTS

8 1/2 ounces of flour
1/2 teaspoon of salt
1 1/2 tablespoons of sugar
1 egg yolk
5 1/2 ounces of softened butter
1/2 cup of ice water

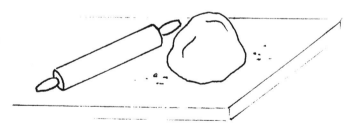

MAKES 1 PIE CRUST

EMERALD SOUP

(1) Wilt the onion in 1 tablespoon of butter or olive oil.

(2) Add boiling consumé and the zucchini.

(3) After 5 or 6 minutes, add the sorrel, and cook 3 minutes more.

(4) Add the spinach leaves, flat parsley, fresh tarragon, and cook 3 minutes more.

(5) Use a hand blender to purée all the ingredients in the pot.

(6) Remove from heat. Add the sour cream. Return to heat and bring to a boil.

(7) Pour into a soup tureen or individual soup plates. Add a few slices of hard-boiled egg and chives to each plate. Serve.

▨ INGREDIENTS

2 spring onions, coursely chopped
1 tablespoon of butter or olive oil
5 cups of beef consumé
1 zucchini cut into small chunks
1/2 cup of sorrel leaves, torn into pieces
1 cup of spinach leaves, stemmed and torn into 2 or 3 pieces
parsley, snipped
tarragon, snipped
5 tablespoons of sour cream
hard-boiled egg for garnish
chives, snipped

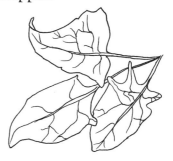

SERVES 4

A NORDIC PICK OF THE
GARDEN SUMMER SOUP

(1) In a large pot, cook the onion in a little butter and olive oil until just pale-gold.

(2) Add the boiling water and all vegetables; then add the sugar (Scandinavian touch) and simmer for 30-35 minutes. Mix with a hand blender directly into the pot.

(3) Add salt and pepper to taste.

(4) Add 6 cups of hot milk and the pommade of butter and flour (the roux).

(5) Cook slowly for a few minutes, stirring well. Then take the pot off of the heat, and add 2 tablespoons of buterr and chopped parsley. Serve.

▨ INGREDIENTS

2 cups of onions, sliced and coarsely chopped

butter and olive oil for onions

5 cups of boiling water

2 cups of zucchini in chunks

2 cups of green beans strung and cut into thirds

2 cups of diced potatoes

1 cup of carrots, sliced

1 tablespoon of sugar

salt and pepper to taste

6 cups of hot milk

2 tablespoons of butter, softened; and 2 tablespoons of flour, worked with fingers into a pommade

2 tablespoons of butter, added with the parsley

flat parsley, chopped

SERVES 4

WATERCRESS AND ZUCCHINI
SOUP

NOTE: *To eat hot or chilled.*

(1) In a large pot, heat 1 tablespoon of butter and 1 tablespoon of olive oil. Add the leek and onion; and fry over low heat for about 2 minutes. Stir until onion and leek are golden.

(2) Add 4 cups of consumé, zucchini chunks, and watercress. Bring to a boil and simmer for 5 minutes.

(3) Add potatoes. Reduce heat and cook for 35 minutes.

(4) Purée with a hand blender directly into the pot.

(5) Strain soup to remove any strings from the water cress.

(6) Return soup to the pot. Add milk, cream, and 1/4 stick butter. Stir well and adjust seasoning.

(7) Place 2 or 3 leaves of watercress without the stems on top of each soup bowl. Serve hot or cold.

INGREDIENTS

1 tablespoon of butter
1 tablespoon of olive oil
1 large leek, sliced, white part only
1 onion, sliced
4 cups of chicken consumé
1 zucchini cut into chunks
2 bunches of watercress
4 potatoes, peeled and sliced or cubed
1 cup of milk
1 cup of heavy cream
1/4 stick of butter
salt and pepper to taste

SERVES 8

A SOUP WITH THE PERFUME AND FLAVOR OF PROVENCE

(1) Warm several tablespoons of olive oil in a large pot or sauce pan. Add onions, leeks and celery. Sauté gently with an occasional stir until lightly colored. Add the diced tomato. Stir. About 7 minutes in all.

(2) Pour in 8 cups of boiling water. Add the bouillon cube and the diced zucchini. Cook approximately 20 minutes over medium heat.

(3) Liquefy the solids with a food processor. (I like using a hand-held mixer that can go directly into the pot.)

(4) Pour the boiling hot soup over 3 or 4 tablespoons of the PISTOU (quantity depends on personal taste) placed in bottom of a tureen. Test for seasoning. Add to the tureen the grated Gruyère and the bread which has been toasted, buttered and broken into pieces.

(5) Ladle into individual bowls. Sprinkle with chopped parsley and grated Parmesan. Serve.

PISTOU

2 large handfuls of fresh basil, leaves only
garlic (addicts have been known to go up to 6 cloves)
a few grains of sea salt
1/2 cup of olive oil, extra virgin, add more if needed

(1) Pound the basil leaves and the peeled cloves of garlic in a large mortar. Pounding in a few grains of sea salt (Kosher salt) will keep the basil green. Slowly, add the olive oil. Stir well. The result should be a thick purée.

(2) The PISTOU can be made in a blender or food processor although the flavor and texture won't be quite the same.

NOTE: PISTOU *can be made only with fresh basil. The aroma of the PISTOU conjures up conviviality and happy days in the sun.*

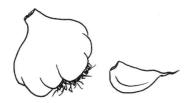

NOTE: *In the South of France, "pistou" is the kissing cousin to the Pesto of Italy. Add a dollop of "pistou" in soup, on pasta, or on a baked potato and grace the "daily daily" with a touch of the sublime. To make sure your life will be so blessed, grow a pot of basil on your window sill.... just in case your local grocery can't supply it.*

▨ INGREDIENTS

2 onions, sliced fine
2 leeks, sliced fine; white part only
2 stalks of celery, sliced fine
3 large ripe tomatoes, peeled, seeded, diced
8 cups of water, boiling
1 bouillon cube
2 zucchini, diced

PISTOU (see adjacent page)

1/4 pound of Gruyère cheese, grated
6-8 slices of slightly stale bread, toasted, buttered, and broken into pieces
olive oil
salt and pepper
flat parsley
Parmesan cheese, grated

SERVES 6-8

DANIEL BOULUD'S
ZUCCHINI AND SHRIMP APPETIZER

(1) Sauté the zucchini and shrimp in olive oil over high heat or 3 to 4 minutes.
(2) Add the orange peel, basil, salt, and pepper.
(3) Heat through, 1 to 2 minutes then discard the orange peel.
(4) Serve topped with orange segments and drizzled with olive oil.

NOTE: *Daniel Boulud, owner of two restaurants in New York, is one of the most acclaimed French-born chefs in America. His cuisine reflects the smiling lightness of his personality.*

▨ INGREDIENTS

1 cup of sliced zucchini
1 pound of shrimp, peeled and deveined
olive oil
3 pieces of orange peel
10 leaves of basil, torn into pieces
1 or 2 oranges sectioned into segments
salt and pepper to taste

SERVES 6-8

TAGLIATELLE
WITH SHRIMP AND ZUCCHINI

(1) Heat oil in a large skillet. Add crushed garlic. Cook about 30 seconds and discard.

(2) Add zucchini and cook for 2 minutes over medium-high heat.

(3) Add the shrimp, salt, pepper, and a pinch of peperoncino and cook 3 minutes, tossing constantly.

(4) Have ready a large pot of salted boiling water. A tablespoon of olive oil will keep the pasta from sticking.

(5) Add pasta to pot. Cook 2 or 3 minutes. Test that they are cooked but still "al dente."

(6) Drain. Return pasta to pot with the shrimp and zucchini. Add a good lump of butter, salt, pepper, and Parmesan. Rush to table. Each guest can add more butter and Parmesan according to taste.

NOTE: *Butter and cheese with shellfish is regarded as an iconoclasm by the purists. But we love it that way and so do our friends.*

▨ INGREDIENTS

olive oil and crushed garlic for skillet

1/2 pound of zucchini, cut into 1/4-inch matchsticks

1/2 pounds of shrimp, shelled and cut in half

salt and pepper to taste

peperoncino

olive oil

1 pound of tagliatelle (egg pasta)

flat parsley

grated Parmesan cheese

butter

NOTE: *Pasta made with eggs cook with great rapidity. Zucchini and shrimp are a particularly happy combination. Sautéed zucchini matchsticks and pasta without the shrimp work out beautifully too. In which case add a handful of chopped parsley at time of the final toss.*

SERVES 6

CAESAR'S SAUCE

NOTE: In Caesar's Rome, your spit roasted duck or pheasant might have been served with a sweet and sour sauce somewhat like this.

(1) Combine the chicken stock, duck juice, honey, vinegar, and zucchini in a pot.
(2) Add the thyme, celery seed, and pepper; then bring to a boil.
(3) Thicken with a little flour or roux.
(4) Pour over the duck or pheasant before serving.

NOTE: A Roman cook might have tossed some chopped chicken or duck livers into the sauce.

▨ INGREDIENTS

2 cups of chicken stock
1 cup of the juices from the roasting duck, skimmed of its fat
1 tablespoon of honey
1 dash of wine vinegar
1 zucchini, cut into cubes
1/2 teaspoon of thyme
1/2 teaspoon of celery seed
1/2 teaspoon of black pepper corns, ground to a powder
1/2 cup of flour for thickening sauce, if desired

A STIR FRY

(1) Lightly fry the chicken strips in a heated Teflon-lined pan with the peanut oil. Stir until golden.
(2) Arrange chicken and vegetables on each plate.
(3) Sprinkle the nuts and the onion over the chicken strips and add a few tufts of parsley. Serve.

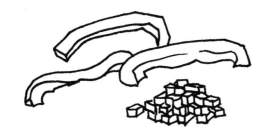

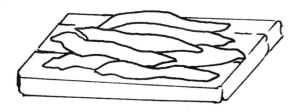

▨ INGREDIENTS

4 chicken breasts, boneless, cut into strips
1 tablespoon of peanut oil
1 carrot, thinly sliced
1 small zucchini, thinly sliced
1 small green pepper, cut in strips, then diced
parsley for garnish

TOPPING

2 small onions, thinly sliced
2 tablespoons of coarsely chopped unsalted peanuts or cashews

(1) Dry out the onion rings in a slow oven.
(2) Dry out the nuts in a slow oven, set aside.

SERVES 4

A TENDER MELTING SOUFFLÉ
WITH A CREAMY TOMATO PURÉE

(1) Slice zucchini coin thin. Sauté gently in butter and oil just to color.

(2) Purée in a food processor.

(3) Melt butter in sauce pan over low heat. Gradually stir in flour, adding milk, little-by-little. Season with salt, pepper, and grated nutmeg.

(4) Stir in grated cheese. Remove from heat. Beat in egg yolks, one-by-one, then add the zucchini purée from the food processor.

(5) Whip egg whites stiff. Add 1/4 to lighten mass. Fold in remainder of the beaten whites.

(6) Transfer to a quart soufflé mold, buttered and dusted with grated cheese and bread crumbs.

(7) Set into lower third of preheated 400°F. oven. After 10 minutes reduce heat to 350°F. and bake 15 minutes more. The interior should still be creamy.

(8) Serve immediately with a side bowl of tomato purée.

▨ INGREDIENTS

1 pound of small to medium zucchini
butter and olive oil for step (1)
3 tablespoons of butter
3 tablespoons of flour
1 cup of milk
salt and pepper to taste
nutmeg, grated
1 cup of grated Gruyère cheese + 1/2
   cup for dusting with bread crumbs
4 egg yolks
5 egg whites
bread crumbs
Tomato Purée (see next column)

NOTE: *A beautiful arrangement of pink
   and pale green*

NOTE: *If using tinned tomatoes, press
   out the maximum juice.*

SERVES 4

Tomato Purée

olive oil
1 onion, small, cut into chunks
6 leaves of fresh basil
1 cup of tomato purée (1-pound tin
   of Italian tomatoes, drained or 1
   pound of fresh tomatoes, quartered)
pinch of sugar
salt and pepper to taste
1 cup of thick cream.

(1) Warm 1 tablespoon of olive oil in
   a heavy sauce pan. Add the onion,
   then sauté until translucent.
(2) Add basil. Add the fresh tomatoes
   quartered or the drained tinned
   tomatoes with a pinch of sugar.
(3) Cook over low heat partially
   covered for approximately 30
   minutes. Season with salt and
   pepper.
(4) Pass through a food mill or press
   through a sieve.
(5) Mix with the cream and serve
   with the Soufflé.

CANDIDA'S SHRIMP
AND ZUCCHINI RISOTTO

(1) Shell and de-vein shrimp. Cut in 3 or 4 pieces. Depends on size. Hold aside.

(2) Pound the shells. Toss them into 3 cups of water. Bring to a boil. Keep in readiness.

(3) Color lightly in olive oil the diced zucchini and the diced celery. Hold aside.

(4) In a another pot, warm the diced onion in 1 tablespoon of butter and 1 tablespoon of olive oil. Add the rice and with a wooden spoon, turn until each grain is coated.

(5) Add the simmering fish stock, 1/4-cup at a time. Stir constantly. As the rice absorbs the liquid, slowly pour on more of the fish stock.

(6) After 15 minutes, add the zucchini, celery, and shrimp. Continue to cook and stir for another 5 minutes while adding more stock.

(7) Risotto should be done in approximately 20 minutes. Remove from heat. Add butter, Parmesan, parsley, salt, and pepper. Vigorous stirring at this point will make the risotto even creamier. For each serving, sprinkle with grated Parmesan and add a nut of fresh butter.

NOTE: *A lovely dish for a tête à tête. The second party sits in the kitchen to watch while you stir.*

NOTE: For a flavorful fish stock, pound the shrimp shells and boil them in 3 cups of water. Strain before using. Because risotto requires constant stirring, all ingredients should be at hand ready to pour into the pot as needed.

▩ INGREDIENTS

1 medium zucchini, diced
1/4 pound of shrimp, peeled, deveined, and cut into 3 or 4 pieces
1 small onion or shallot, finely chopped
1 rib of celery, diced
3 cups of consommé or fish stock
3/4 cup of round grain rice, Arborio or Carnaroli
3 tablespoons of butter
olive oil
1/2 cup of grated Parmesan
flat parsley, chopped
at table... fresh butter and grated Parmesan

SERVES 2

FRITTATA

(1) Salt the zucchini to draw off the water. After 30 minutes, pat dry.
(2) Cook onion in olive oil until translucent. Add zucchini. Cook for 5 minutes
(3) Transfer to a large bowl. Add spinach and diced tomato. Mix well.
(4) Beat eggs with a fork. Add generous amounts of herbs–chopped parsley, snipped chives, torn leaves of basil.
(5) Combine the eggs with the vegetable mixture. Pour into a 10-inch skillet in which you have melted 2 tablespoons of butter.
(6) Cook over low heat slowly, slowly until bottom is set. About 15 minutes. The top should still be slightly runny.
(7) The tricky part is next. Smartly turn over the frittata on to a large pot lid. Slide back in the pan. (For security it is wise to stand by the sink during this maneuver.) Cook an additional 15-20 seconds. Cut in wedges and serve at once. Sprinkle with a little grated Parmesan.

▨ INGREDIENTS

3 medium zucchini, cut lengthwise
1 large onion, sliced
3 tablespoons of olive oil
10-15 leaves of young spinach, cooked just until wilted
1 large red tomato, peeled, seeded, diced
5 large eggs
generous amounts of parsley, chives, and basil
2 tablespoons of butter
salt and pepper to taste

NOTE: The Italian frittata is robust and hearty. Although high and cooked on both sides, it should not be dry within. All combinations are possible.
NOTE: Rather than turn over the frittata, place under broiler until top is set.

SERVES 4

A ZUCCHINI EGG FU YUNG

Main course for lunch or light supper

(1) Sauté chicken pieces in peanut oil for 45 seconds. Add celery, zucchini, and onion. Simmer 30 to 45 seconds then add soy sauce. Cook 30 seconds more. Set aside.

(2) Prepare the sauce. Heat 1 tablespoon of peanut oil. Add Shiitake mushroom. Cook 45 seconds. Add 1 tablespoon of soy sauce and 1 teaspoon of sugar. Cook 15 seconds. Add 3/4 cups chicken broth and bring to a boil.

(3) Reduce heat, Stir while gradually adding cornstarch dissolved in water. Set aside but keep warm.

(4) Stir eggs in a bowl. Add salt and the zucchini-chicken mixture into the eggs. Pour into heavy pan, the bottom spread with 1 tablespoon of warmed peanut oil. Reduce heat and cook until underside is golden brown. Lift bottom occasionally to avoid sticking or burning.

(5) Use spatula to fold over the omelet and slide on to plate. Pour on the reheated sauce. Garnish with parsley and slivered ham.

▧ INGREDIENTS

1 chicken breast cut in pieces (1/4 pound)
1 tablespoon of peanut oil
1 large rib celery, cut in diagonal slices
1 medium zucchini, cut in diagonal slices
1 spring onion or 1 shallot cut in lengthwise slices
1 tablespoon of soy sauce
4 large eggs
1/4 teaspoon of salt

FOR THE SAUCE

1 tablespoon of peanut oil
3 dried Shiitake mushrooms, soaked in warm water. When plumped up, squeeze dry and cut each into six slices
1 tablespoon of soy sauce
1 teaspoon of sugar
3/4 cup of chicken broth
1 heaping teaspoon of cornstarch dissolved in 2 tablespoons of water
2 teapoons of chopped parsley
3 tablespoons of slivered ham

SERVES 2-3

CHOUKCHOUKA

(1) Dice zucchini, carrot, celery, onion and tomato.
(2) Gently sauté onion in 1 tablespoon of peanut oil and 1 tablespoon of olive oil for 3 or 4 minutes.
(3) Add zucchini, carrot, celery, and tomato with basil and parsley. Cook slowly for 5 or 6 minutes. Season with salt and pepper.
(4) Press two depressions into the vegetables, using the back of a tablespoon. Carefully crack, then slide an egg into each of the depressions. Cover the pan and cook until the whites are set. The yolks, however, should remain soft. They are delicious dribbling over the vegetables.

NOTE: For Those Who Like It Hot, imitate the Tunisians with a light dusting of paprika and a pinch of cayenne

▨ INGREDIENTS

1 zucchini
1 carrot
1 stalk of celery
1 onion
1 tomato
peanut oil, olive oil
basil, parsley
2 eggs
salt and pepper to taste
Parmesan, grated (optional)

NOTE: A great meal in a single dish from Tunisia

SERVES 2 (but can be multiplied *ad infinitum*)

AN ENTERTAINING
ZUCCHINI GRATIN

(1) Mix together in a large bowl, zucchini, onions, eggs, parsley, dill, mint, Gruyère, Feta, and seasonings.
(2) Gradually stir in the flour.
(3) Pour into a buttered square or rectangular pan and smooth the top. This may be prepared ahead of time.
(4) Before setting in oven, sprinkle the surface with bread crumbs and grated Gruyère. Dot with butter and decorate with pitted olives.
(5) Bake in a moderate oven for approximately 30 to 35 minutes.
(6) Cut into squares for serving.

NOTE: *A perfect dish for a buffet, inspired by Turkish hostesses who entertain on the grand scale.*

▨ INGREDIENTS

6 small zucchini, grated
2 medium onions or 5 scallions, finely chopped
3 eggs, lightly beaten
1/2 cup of flat parsley, chopped
1/2 cup of dill, chopped
1/2 cup of fresh mint, chopped
1 cup of grated Gruyère
2 ounces of Feta cheese, crumbled
salt, pepper, and cayenne to taste
1 1/2 cups of flour

TOPPING
1/2 cup dried bread crumbs
1/2 cup grated Gruyère
4 tablespoons of butter
black olives to decorate

ACCOMPANIMENT
A bowl of thick natural yogurt generously sprinkled with chopped fresh mint

SERVES 8-10

SURPRISES BAKED IN A PIE

Prepare the pastry:

(1) Cut butter into the flour with two knives, or work the butter little by little into the flour with finger tips.

(2) Gradually add just enough ice water to form a soft dough that holds together. Do not overwork.

(3) Wrap in wax paper or foil and chill for half an hour.

Prepare the béchamel sauce:

(4) Melt the butter over low heat. Gradually stir in the flour.

(5) Add warm milk in stages. Stir continuously until béchamel is thick.

(6) Season with salt, pepper, nutmeg.

Final preparation:

(7) Fry the zucchini slices in vegetable oil until golden on both sides. Drain and set aside.

(8) Lightly fry the onion and garlic in olive oil. Add mushrooms then stir over heat.

(9) Add white wine. Let evaporate. Pemove from heat.

(10) Mix mushrooms, onions, parsley, mint, thyme, basil, and ham into cooled béchamel.

(11) Fit 2/3 of the pastry dough into bottom and sides of a 10-inch spring pan.

(12) Spread a layer of tagliatelle, a layer of zucchini, and a layer of the enriched béchamel. Sprinkle with Parmesan. Repeat this order until you reach the top of cake pan.

(13) Poll out remaining dough to form a lid to cover the timbale. Prick with fork. Brush with beaten egg.

(14) Set in preheated hot oven. Bake 10 minutes. Reduce oven to moderate. Bake 30 minutes or until crust is golden. Remove sides of spring pan. Present the free-standing timbale. Cut into wedges and serve.

⊞ INGREDIENTS

6 medium zucchini, sliced lengthwise 1/8-inch thick

2 tablespoons of finely chopped
onion

1 clove of garlic, minced

3 tablespoons of olive oil in which
to fry onion, garlic, and mushrooms

1 pound of mushrooms

2 tablespoons of white wine

1 bunch of flat parsley, minced

6 large leaves of mint, cut into ribbons

1 teaspoon of fresh thyme or 1/2
teaspoon of dried thyme

6 large leaves of basil, torn into
small pieces

3/4 pound ham, cubed

10 ounces of green tagliatelle (flat
spinach noodles) cooked al dente
and drained

1/2 cup of grated Parmesan

THE PASTRY

2 1/2 cups of flour sifted with 1
teaspoon of salt

12 tablespoons of very cold butter

3 to 4 tablespoons of ice water

BECHAMEL SAUCE

3 tablespoon of butter

3 tablespoon of flour

2 cups of milk

salt to taste

freshly ground pepper

pinch of freshly grated nutmeg

*NOTE: This was one of Candida's
fantasy flights. It turned out to be
spectacular. Basically it is an
assembly job. Not hard. But
does take time. Instead of the
ham, it might be fun to experiment with tiny meat balls.*

SERVES 8-10

CANDIDA'S ZUCCHINI
ALLA PARMIGIANA

(1) Cut the zucchini into long, thin, flexible slices.

(2) Dredge slices first in flour, then in beaten egg. Tap off excess.

(3) Shallow fry slices in hot vegetable oil until both sides are golden. Salt and pepper as you go. Drain on kitchen paper.

(4) Chop finely onion, basil and parsley Cook gently in warm olive oil in large frying pan. About 10 minutes. Set aside.

(5) Stew the quartered tomatoes in their own juice. About 15 minutes. Pass through a vegetable mill to remove skins.

(6) Add tomatoes to onion mixture in the large frying pan. Season with salt, pepper.

(7) In another frying pan, gently sauté the meat in warmed olive oil. Separate the meat into crumbles with fork and cook until it loses its rosiness.

(8) Add white wine and let it evaporate over medium heat.

(9) Butter an oven-ware pan. Place a layer of zucchini, a layer of tomato sauce, a layer of meat, a sprinkle of Parmesan. Repeat layers. At half mark, dot with bits of mozzarella. Top level should be tomato sauce, Parmesan and pieces of mozzarella. Bake 15 to 18 minutes in hot oven.

NOTE: An Absolute "must."

NOTE: A dish usually associated with eggplant, becomes far more delicate when made with zucchini. Quite irresistible.

Candida manages to cut 8 thin slices from a medium zucchini by holding it in her left hand towards her heart like a dagger and with a sharp knife cutting a 1/8th slice while slowly drawing the blade towards her. From the second slice on, it gets easier.

▧ INGREDIENTS

2 pounds of zucchini
3 to 4 large eggs
3/4 pounds of ground beef
1/2 cup of white wine
flour for dredging
peanut oil for frying
TOMATO SAUCE
1 small onion
2 pounds of Italian plum tomatoes, quartered
10 to 12 leaves basil, torn
   generous handful of flat parsley
      salt, pepper
         olive oil
      3/4 cup Parmesan, grated
3/4 cup mozzarella

SERVES 6-8

TUNA-FILLED ZUCCHINI

(1) Blanch zucchini for five minutes. Drain. Cut off tips then slice in half lengthwise.

(2) Hollow zucchini halves. Turn upside down to drain. Squeeze dry only six of the zucchini centers.

(3) Chop centers finely and combine with tuna fish, chopped almonds, Parmesan, diced tomatoes, parsley, basil, thyme, salt, and pepper.

(4) Moisten the mixture with olive oil. Spoon into the zucchini shells lined up in a buttered baking pan.

(5) Sprinkle with bread crumbs. Dot with butter.

(6) Bake in a 350°F. oven for 30 minutes. Serve.

NOTE: *Popular in Tuscany.*

▣ INGREDIENTS

8 zucchini

1/4 cup of canned tuna, flaked with a fork,

1 dozen almonds, shelled, skinned and cut in small pieces, not ground

1/4 cup of Parmesan

2 Italian plum tomatoes, peeled, seeded, diced

2 tablespoons of flat parsley minced

1 tablespoon of basil, torn

pinch of thyme

salt and pepper

1 tablespoons of olive oil

grated bread crumbs

3 tablespoons of butter

accompany with Candida's "No Cook" piquant Tomato Sauce (see page 48)

SERVES 4-6

ZUCCHINI TREATED LIKE A NAPOLEON

(1) Steam the zucchini for about 18-20 minutes. They should retain their form.
(2) Slice horizontally into 3 equal parts. Save the cap which will be replaced as a lid.
(3) Spread each layer with a little *Ratatouille*.
(4) Reform each zucchini. Replace the lid on top.
(5) Set on individual plates. Frame with a wreath of *Pistou*.

NOTE: For a sophisticated starter.

▧ INGREDIENTS

4 round zucchini
Ratatouille (see page 50)
Pistou (see page 28)

NOTE: This pretty entrée is a favorite with a group of young Paris caterers.

SERVES 4

CANDIDA'S "NO-COOK"
PIQUANT TOMATO SAUCE

(1) Combine all ingredients in a
blender. If sauce seems too liquid,
Candida thickens it with a few
Grissini which she has grated into
crumbs.

NOTE: *The crunch of the almonds in the
filling and the kick of the peperoncini
in the sauce transform a perfectly
nice dish into "A Something Special."*

▣ INGREDIENTS

4 Italian plum tomatoes, peeled
   and seeded (Preferably sun-
   kissed)
1/4 small onion, grated
2 tablespoons of flat parsley,
   minced
10 leaves of basil, torn into
   small pieces
pinch of fresh thyme
1 garlic clove, minced
1/8 teaspoon of Italian peperoncini but beware this is hot
   stuff
1 tablespoons of olive oil
salt

SERVES 6

MOUSSAKA

(1) Cut zucchini into 1/3-inch slices. Dust with flour. Fry lightly in peanut oil. Drain on absorbent paper. Set aside.

(2) Fry chopped onion in olive oil until translucent. Add ground lamb. Poke it around and cook gently until the pink disappears.

(3) Add chopped tomatoes, cinnamon, oregano, salt, and pepper. Cook for 20 minutes.

(4) Remove from heat. Add parsley and 1 beaten egg. Mix well. Add just enough bread crumbs to hold mixture together.

(5) In a large buttered square or rectangular baking pan, place a layer of zucchini slices, then a layer of meat mixture. Repeat.

(6) Top with a thick layer of Enriched Béchamel made by combining the listed ingredients. Bake in moderate oven (300 F.) for 20 to 25 minutes until golden brown. Let rest at room temperature 10 to 15 minutes before cutting into squares.

NOTE: A Standby in Greece and all countries along the Eastern Mediterranean.

▨ INGREDIENTS

6 medium zucchini
flour for dusting
peanut oil
1 large onion, chopped
olive oil
1 pound of ground lamb
3 tomatoes, peeled and chopped
1/4 teaspoon of cinnamon
pinch of oregano
salt and pepper to taste
parsley, chopped
1 egg
bread crumbs

Enriched BECHAMEL

3 tablespoons of butter
3 tablespoons of flour
2 cups of milk
nutmeg to taste
salt and pepper to taste
3/4 grated cheese. (Parmesan and or Gruyère or both)
2 eggs

NOTE:The slather of rich Béchamel is Greek as Zorba.

SERVES 4-6

RATATOUILLE

(1) Set up a pretty table under a tree and arrange to eat outdoors on a dreamy summer's day.

(2) Line up 4 bowls. An orderly progression is the secret.

(3) Into Bowl 1, place the peppers and onions cut into small squares.
Into Bowl 2, place the peeled eggplant cut into 1-inch cubes.
Into Bowl 3, place the unpeeled zucchini cut into 1-inch cubes.
Into Bowl 4, place the peeled tomatoes, seeded, quartered, and sprinkled with thyme.
You are now in business.

(4) Pour 3 tablespoons of olive oil into each of two pans. Warm the olive oil. Onions and peppers go into Pan A. Season with salt and pepper. Cook gently over low heat for 15 minutes.

(5) Into Pan B place the tomatoes. Cook over high heat...3 minutes. Drain extra oil from both pans. Hold aside the peppers, onions, and tomatoes.

(5) Warm 5 tablespoons of olive oil in a large skillet. Sauté the eggplant cubes until golden, about 7-8 minutes. Remove the eggplant and set aside. In the same skillet, add a little fresh olive oil if needed and sauté the cubes of zucchini, about 7-8 minutes.
Drain zucchini and set aside.

(6) Everything is now ready for the "Let's Go" signal. Transfer all the elements into a Dutch oven (including orange peel and optional hot, red pepper). Stir lightly with a wooden spoon to mix. Add crushed garlic. Reheat gently 15 to 20 minutes. After 10 minutes add parsley and scissored ribbons of basil. Test seasoning, adding salt and pepper as desired.

NOTE: *Time was when ratatouille was cooked to a mush. We hated it. Styles have changed. Lesser cooking time means each vegetable retains its shape and individuality.*

NOTE: *This celebrated "mess of vegetables" may be eaten hot or cold. It may be worked into an omelet or it may be used as the filling of our ZUCCHINI NAPOLEON. It is a main course accompaniment or an hors d'oeuvre.*

NOTE: *The legendary dish of the sunshine cuisine of Nice.*

▨ INGREDIENTS

2 bell peppers, 1 red and 1 green
3 medium onions, sliced
eggplant
8-10 small zucchini, unpeeled
2 pounds of Italian plum tomatoes, peeled, seeded and quartered
thyme
olive oil...to be dosed as needed
a spiral of dried orange peel
garlic, crushed
Bouquet garni: flat parsley, bay leaf, rosemary, thyme
1/2 cup of chopped parsley
1 cup of fresh basil leaves
salt and pepper

(optional)
1 small, hot, red pepper, seeds removed

SERVES 8-10

ZUCCHINI STUFFED
WITH LAMB AND RICE

(1) Slice off the ends of zucchini Save one end to be a cap. Hollow zucchini leaving 1/4-inch wall.

(2) Mix all ingredients together (except the cooking juice) and pack into the zucchini until about 1/2 inch from tops so that the rice will have room to swell.

(3) Cap the zucchini with the reserved ends.

(4) Set close to each other upright in a deep pot. The zucchini should be close enough to support each other.

(5) Pour on the already prepared cooking juice to just below the top of the zucchini. If necessary, add a little more water.

(6) Bring to boil. Check for seasoning. Cover pot and reduce heat. Simmer until rice is tender.

(7) Drain liquid from pot into saucepan, skim off any fat.

(8) Remove zucchini to individual plates. Pour some of the reheated liquid over each. Serve.

✦ INGREDIENTS

10 small zucchini
1 pound of ground lamb
1 to 1 1/2 cups of canned tomatoes, thoroughly drained of juice
2 tablespoons of tomato paste
2 tablespoons of finely diced green pepper
1/2 teaspoon of allspice, paprika, cayenne, salt, and pepper
1/4 cup of long grain rice

COOKING JUICE

1/2 cup tomato juice
3 tablespoons of lemon juice
Salt
1 1/2 to 2 cups water

NOTE: *This is common to all the Middle East.*

SERVES 4-6

ANTON MOSIMANN'S
STUFFED ZUCCHINI

(1) Shell and devein the shrimp. Flake the crabmeat Roughly chop the water chestnuts.

(2) Spoon out centers of zucchini. (Put aside to use later.)

(3) Place shrimp, crab, chestnuts, egg and sesame oil in food processor. Pulse to a smooth paste. Check for salt and pepper. Incorporate spring onions. Fill the hollowed zucchini.

(4) Sweat shallots, garlic, and ginger in olive oil. Add to vegetable stock. Bring to boil.

(5) Set stuffed zucchini in the liquid. Simmer gently for 15 minutes. Add leeks and carrot to liquid. Cook 5 minutes more. Lift out the zucchini and keep warm.

(6) Reduce liquid. Thicken with cornstarch. Add soy sauce to taste. Coat zucchini with the sauce. Garnish with leek and carrot. Sprinkle with coriander. Serve.

NOTE: *Typical of Mosimann's, always stylish.*

▣ INGREDIENTS

1/4 pound of large shrimp
4 ounces of crab meat
4 water chestnuts
8 medium zucchini (round would be particularly suitable)
1 small egg
1 tablespoons of sesame oil
2 tablespoons of finely chopped spring onions
2 peeled, chopped shallots
1 clove garlic, crushed
1 teaspoon of finely chopped fresh ginger
olive oil
2 1/2 cups of vegetable stock
1/4 pound of leeks, cut into rings
1 medium carrot, finely sliced
1 teaspoon of cornstarch, soy sauce, and fresh coriander, chopped

NOTE: *Mosimann's Club is one of London's top restaurants.*

SERVES 6

VEGETABLE STOCK

(1) Chop finely onion, leek, celery, fennel, cabbage, and tomato. Keep each vegetable separate for the moment.

(2) Heat vegetable oil in a large pan. Sweat onion and leek for 4-5 minutes. Add the remaining vegetables. Sweat for another 10 minutes.

(3) Add 4 cups of water, the small clove, and the bay leaf. Simmer for 20 minutes.

(4) Strain through fine sieve or cloth. Allow to drip. Season with salt and pepper. Use immediately. Can be refrigerated or frozen in small containers.

▣ INGREDIENTS

1 1/2 ounces of onion
1 1/2 ounces of leek
3/4 ounces of celery
3/4 ounce of fennel
1 1/4 ounces of cabbage
1 1/4 ounces of tomato
2 tablespoons of vegetable oil
4 cups of water
1 small clove
1/2 bay leaf
salt and pepper to taste

MAKES ABOUT 4 CUPS

A MOROCCAN GARLIC
CHICKEN WITH ZUCCHINI

(1) Peel ten cloves of garlic.
(2) Fry them to light gold in a Dutch oven with peanut oil.
(3) Add the chicken pieces. Brown on all sides.
(4) Add water, salt, curcuma, and pepper. Bring to the boil.
(5) Cover. Reduce heat. Cook over low heat about 1 hour. Turn chicken pieces from time to time.
(6) Remove chicken. Add to the sauce, the zucchini, the coriander. Salt to taste. Cook gently 20 minutes then return chicken to pot to reheat.

▩ INGREDIENTS

10 garlic cloves, peeled
1 chicken, 3 1/2 pounds cut into 8 pieces
2 tablespoons of peanut oil
2 cups water
1 teaspoon of curcuma
1 tablespoon of salt
black pepper, freshly ground
2 1/4 pounds of medium zucchini, each zucchini cut crosswise into 3 or 4 chunks
1 tablespoon of coriander smashed

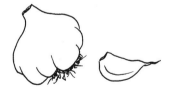

SERVES 6

FARMER'S CASSEROLE

(1) Sauté onions in butter until translucent, set aside.

(2) Brown the meat cubes on all sides in butter

(3) In a deep heavy casserole (iron would be lovely) layer the ingredients as follows: onions, zucchini, green peppers, and tomatoes. Top with meat cubes.

(4) Pour 2 cups of boiling water delicately down sides of casserole taking care not to disturb the layers of vegetables.

(5) Season with black pepper, allspice, salt, and paprika.

(6) Cover the pot. Cook over direct heat. When half cooked, add lemon juice. At end, test again for salt and lemon juice.

Cooking time is approximately 45 minutes.

NOTE: *As an Armenian might do it.*

⊞ INGREDIENTS

2 medium onions, sliced

2 ounces of butter, more if needed

1 pound of boneless lamb, cut into small cubes

2 pounds of zucchini, cubed

2 green peppers, cut into 1-inch squares

3 fresh tomatoes cut into cubes or 2 cups tinned tomatoes, drained and cubed

2 cups of boiling water, set aside

black pepper to taste

1/8 teaspoon of allspice

1/8 teaspoon of paprika

3 tablespoons of lemon juice, more, if needed at end

SERVES 4-6

"PAPOUTSAKIA"
OR BAKED LITTLE SHOES

(1) Scrub the zucchini and boil them for 5 minutes. Drain and dry. Slice off the two ends and cut the zucchini into two halves lengthwise.

(2) Carefully spoon out the centers, leaving a 1/4-inch rim all around.

(3) Salt the interiors and turn the shells upside down to drain. Wipe dry.

(4) Chop the inside flesh of the zucchini and squeeze out the water.

(5) Mix the zucchini innards with bread crumbs, 1/2 cup of cheese, 2 eggs, salt, pepper, and parsley.

(6) Rub olive oil into the walls of the zucchini shells before filling them with the above mixture.

(7) Cover each "Little Shoe" with Enriched Béchamel made by combining the listed ingredients. Dot tops with butter and sprinkle with 1/4-cup cheese.

(8) Bake in moderate oven (300 F.) for 30 minutes.

✦ INGREDIENTS

8 zucchini, 6 inches long
salt to lightly coat the spooned-out zucchini interior
1/2 cup of bread crumbs
1/2 cup of grated cheese (Parmesan or Kefalotiri)
2 eggs
salt and pepper to taste
parsley, generous bunch
olive oil

Enriched Béchamel

4 tablespoons of butter
4 tablespoons of flour
2 cups of milk
nutmeg to taste
salt and pepper to taste
1 egg
1/2 cup of grated cheese (Parmesan and or Gruyère or both) for topping

NOTE: The Greeks call their stuffed zucchini "Little Shoes" Papoutsakia. For the name alone, I am in love with them.

SERVES 4

STIR-FRY PORK
WITH ZUCCHINI AND CRANBERRIES

(1) In a large bowl, mix well the consommé, cornstarch, beaten egg, and flour.
(2) Dip pork cubes into above mixture.
(3) Dice onion, zucchini, and bell pepper. (Oriental cooking is fast but it would help to have six pairs of hands.)
(4) Heat cranberry juice and cranberry jelly over low heat until jelly melts.
(5) Fry pork in very hot peanut oil for 2 minutes.
(6) In a second pan, heat 1 tablespoon of peanut oil. After 20 seconds add diced onions and diced zucchini. Cook 20 seconds more.
(7) Add cranberry juice and melted jelly. Cook 10 seconds. Add cubes of fried pork. Season with salt and pepper. Cook an additional 20 seconds.

NOTE: Total cooking time of this and that and the assembly–3 minutes 10 seconds over high heat.

▨ INGREDIENTS

4 tablespoons of consommé
4 pounds of cornstarch
1 egg, beaten
4 tablespoons of flour
1 pound of lean pork, cut into large cubes
3 1/2 ounces of onion, diced
3 1/2 ounces zucchini, diced
3 1/2 ounces of bell pepper, diced
8 tablespoons of cranberry juice cocktail
5 heaping tablespoons of whole-berry cranberry jelly
peanut oil, salt, and pepper

NOTE: I asked Saigon-born Robert Vifian to dream up an East-West dish. Robert and his brother, Freddy, are the owner-chefs of the Tan Dinh, Paris' top Vietnamese restaurant. "I cook in my tradition," said Robert, "but not necessarily traditional Vietnamese." This dish is like Cape Cod clasping hands with Southeast Asia.

ZUCCHINI BOATS
INDIAN STYLE

(1) Split zucchini lengthwise. Scoop out centers leaving an inch rim all around. Combine the chopped onion, the chopped centers from the zucchini, and the saffron.

(2) Fry in butter for about 5 minutes.

(3) Mix together yogurt, cream, almonds, cardomom, lemon juice, and salt. Add to the chopped zucchini and onions. Cook over gentle heat for another 5 minutes.

(4) Transfer mixture to zucchini shells. Sprinkle a few coriander seeds on each zucchini half and a few grinds of pepper.

(5) Bake in moderate oven for 25 minutes.

▨ INGREDIENTS

2 pounds of zucchini
1 onion, finely chopped
1 pinch of saffron
4 tablespoons of butter
1/4 cup of yogurt
1 cup of heavy cream
5 tablespoons of blanched
    almonds, coarsely chopped
8 cardomom seeds, crushed
1/2 teaspoon of lemon juice
salt to taste
coriander seeds
pepper to taste for topping

NOTE: *This recipe, adapted from Dharam Jit Singh's "Classic Cooking from India" presents zucchini in a guise as different from every day as a trip abroad.*

SERVES 6-8

BREADLESS MINI SANDWICHES

NOTE: *Slices of zucchini clasp a tasty chopped meat filling*

(1) Toast cumin in a dry pan to re-lease flavor. Crush with mortar and pestle.
(2) Season meat with cumin, salt, and pepper.
(3) Cut zucchini crosswise into 1/2-inch lengths. Stand each chunk on end and cut down into 4 equal slices. (Slices should be 1/4-inch thick.)
(4) Press chopped meat between 2 zucchini layers.
(5) Roll in flour. Dip into beaten egg and fry in olive oil until just golden.
(6) Transfer into baking dish. Cover with tomato sauce and bake 10 minutes in a 350°F. oven. Sprinkle with parsley. The proportion of these mini-sandwiches is 1/4-inch for each zucchini slice and 1/2-inch for the meat filling between.

▨ INGREDIENTS

1/8 teaspoon of ground cumin
1 pound of ground beef
salt and pepper to taste
1 pound of small zucchini
flour
2 eggs, beaten
olive oil
tomato sauce
flat parsley, chopped

NOTE: *The cumin makes for taste excitement. However, the difference between powdered cumin, store-bought in a jar, and pounding your own is wide as the world.*

SERVES 6-8

CHINESE PRESTO MAGIC, 5 MINUTES FLAT
ZUCCHINI, MUSHROOMS, SNOW PEAS, HAM

(1) Slice zucchini into 1/4-inch slices, cut on the diagonal.

(2) Slice mushrooms vertically.

(3) Heat oil in a wok over high heat.

(4) Sauté zucchini for 2 minutes.

(5) Sauté mushrooms for 1 minute.

(6) Add snowpeas and ham, sauté for 30 seconds.

(7) Add chicken broth mixed with soy sauce, salt, and pepper. Bring to boil for 1 minute.

(8) Reduce heat. Thicken quickly with cornstarch mixture and stir thoroughly.

(9) Transfer to vegetable dish. Sprinkle with parsley. Serve at once.

⊞ INGREDIENTS

1 1/2 pounds of small zucchini
1/2 pound small mushrooms
4 tablespoons of peanut oil
1/4 pound of snow peas
1 or 2 slices of ham, cut into
   3/4-inch strips
3/4 cup of chicken broth
3 tablespoons of soy sauce
1/2 teaspoon of salt
freshly ground black pepper
4 tablespoons of cornstarch
   mixed with 5 tablespoons of
   ice water
parsley

NOTE: *Takes high heat, a wok, and a quick wrist. A simple and excellent dish. Worth the practice to get it split-second right.*

SERVES 6

ZUCCHINI IN FIESTA

(1) Gently color almonds in a little olive oil over low heat; remove and hold aside.

(2) Add a little more oil to the pan. Cook onions until transparent.

(3) Halve zucchini lengthwise. Remove center pulp. Leave 1/4-inch rim all around. Chop pulp. Season with salt, pepper, and marjoram. Add to onions. Cook for 6 to 7 minutes until zucchini have given up their moisture.

(4) Remove from heat. Stir in the toasted almonds. Spoon mixture into the hollowed zucchini.

(5) Fold tomatoes into yogurt. Spread half over bottom of a baking dish which just holds the zucchini comfortably.

(6) Spoon remainder of tomato-yogurt over the zucchini. Sprinkle surface with dried breadcrumbs. Dribble with olive oil.

(7) Bake in a 300°F. oven for 45 minutes. Serve.

▨ INGREDIENTS

olive oil
1 cup of peeled almonds, quartered by hand (Worth the effort. Makes a difference.)
1 cup onions, chopped fine
4 medium zucchini
salt, pepper
3 tablespoons of chopped fresh marjoram
1 pound of fresh Italian plum tomatoes, peeled and coarsely chopped
1 cup of thick natural yogurt
2 tablespoon of dried bread crumbs

NOTE: *Jeremiah Tower and I were visiting Richard Olney's magic hillside house in Provence. Using ingredients at hand, Jeremiah improvised this dish. Richard liked it so much, he called it "Zucchini in Fiesta."*

SERVES 4

ZUCCHINI SWEET AND SOUR

(1) Slice zucchini crosswise into 1/2-inch slices. Cut in half again. Salt for 30 minutes. Pat dry.
(2) Cook gently in 1 tablespoon of oil.
(3) After 3 minutes, season with black pepper and powdered cinnamon.
(4) Add 4 tablespoons of wine vinegar and 2 tablespoons of sugar. Add pine nuts and raisins Cook for 3 minutes more, stirring continuously. Let cool. Can be stored for 3 days in the refrigerator.

NOTE: A Relish that resembles a Chutney.

INGREDIENTS

2 pounds of zucchini
salt to taste
2 tablespoons of olive oil
l/'4 teaspoon of freshly ground pepper
2 teaspoons of cinnamon
4 tablespoons of wine vinegar
2 tablespoons of sugar
2 tablespoons of pine nuts, lightly toasted
2 tablespoons of raisins

ZUCCHINI
MINT AND MUSHROOMS

(1) Warm garlic in olive oil.
(2) Add zucchini, sliced into thin coins.
(3) Cook for 6 minutes
(4) Add a nut of butter and the sliced mushrooms.
(5) Stir constantly. Season with salt and pepper.
(6) One minute before the finish, toss on the fresh mint. Stir throughout.

▨ INGREDIENTS

1 large clove of garlic
olive oil
4 medium zucchini
butter
1/4 pound of mushrooms, sliced
salt, pepper
1/2 cup of fresh mint leaves, packed

NOTE: Long Chinese chop sticks are ideal instruments for stirring.

SERVES 4

EVERYDAY BUT NOT ORDINARY

(1) Cut zucchini into 1/2-inch slices.

(2) Add butter to a heavy pan. Strew bottom with coarsely chopped onions. Salt the onions.

(3) Add the zucchini on top of the onions. Season with salt and freshly ground pepper.

(4) Cover pan with tightly fitting lid. Cook over low heat for 7 minutes. Remove lid. Cook uncovered for 5 minutes. Stir constantly so zucchini and onions do not stick to the bottom of the pan. Transfer to a heated vegetable dish. Salt to taste and give a healthy dose of chopped parsley. Serve.

▧ INGREDIENTS

2 pounds of zucchini, small
2 tablespoons of butter
1 large onion, 6 ounces, coursely chopped
salt, pepper
flat parsley, chopped

NOTE: Very simple. Very good.

SERVES 6

ZUCCHINI TEAMS UP WITH GARLIC

(1) Cut zucchini into slices 1/4-inch thick.
(2) Warm oil in a 9-inch sauté pan.
(3) Cook zucchini over medium heat for 10 minutes.
(4) Season with salt and pepper. Peel garlic cloves and smash with heel of your hand. Add to zucchini and cook 10 minutes more.
(5) Transfer to a hot serving dish and sprinkle generously with grated Parmesan cheese.

▣ INGREDIENTS

3 pounds of zucchini
2 tablespoons of olive oil
salt and pepper to taste
4 cloves of garlic
3 tablespoons of Parmesan cheese

SERVES 4

AS A PERFECT VEGETABLE
WITH PROVENÇAL BUTTER

(1) Trim off the ends of the zucchini and cut each into 3 or 4 chunks. Pare the edges to form ovals.
(2) Toss the zucchini into boiling salted water. Bring back to the boil. Remove zucchini and drain thoroughly.
(3) Heat the oil. Sauté the zucchini, turning them often so they take on an even golden color.
(4) Reduce the heat. Add a little oil, if necessary, and cover. Continue cooking over moderate heat for about 15 minutes, shaking and turning from time to time.
(5) Drain off all the oil used in the cooking.
(6) Add the Provençal Butter already prepared, at intervals. Roll the zucchini ovals in the butter and toss them so they will be well covered. Put a lid on the pan for a few seconds and allow the zucchini to heat up without sputtering. Turn into a heated vegetable dish, adding salt. Serve.

▨ INGREDIENTS

3 pounds of medium zucchini, more or less the same size
5 tablespoons of peanut oil
Provençal Butter (See adjacent page)

NOTE: *This method of detailed simplicity is from my friend Louisette Bertholle who was one of the three authors of* Mastering the Art of French Cooking *before going off to write books on her own.*

SERVES 6

PROVENÇAL BUTTER

(1) Use a fork to work the butter with all the other ingredients until you achieve a homogenous product with the consistence of a pommade. This marvelous butter with its evocations of Provence goes well with almost everything

▨ INGREDIENTS

5 tablespoons of fresh butter
2 shallots passed through a garlic press
1 or 2 garlic cloves passed through a garlic press and then pounded with a pestle
1 tablespoons of olive oil (Remove the germ in the garlic clove if necessary.)
2 tablespoons of fresh herbs chopped fine...chervil, flat parsley, tarragon, basil, whatever is at hand
salt
freshly ground pepper

MAKES ABOUT 5 TABLESPOONS

ANTOINE BOUTERIN'S LEEK AND ZUCCHINI
SUPER-PANCAKE

(1) Cut off the ends of the leek. Remove the papery outer layer. Make four or six slits halfway down. Douse in a bowl of water to flush out any lurking dirt. Dry well.

(2) Julienne the zucchini at 2-inch lengths. Adjust the width to 3/16th of an inch. Squeeze dry in your hands.

(3) In a 8 or 9-inch frying pan, warm the oil. Add the leek and zucchini with the egg, beaten. Add chopped parsley, salt, and pepper (pinch of thyme, optional).

(4) Cook on both sides over medium-low heat. Serve as the vegetable accompaniment.

▣ INGREDIENTS

1 medium leek
1 medium zucchini
2 tablespoons of olive oil
1 egg
flat parsley, chopped, 1 table-spoon
pinch of thyme, optional
salt and pepper to taste

NOTE: *Antoine Bouterin's restaurant in New York often serves dishes he knew growing up in St. Rémy-de-Provence.*

SERVES 2

POGREONSKI

(1) Cut eggplants, zucchini, and tomatoes into chunks.
(2) Mince the garlic and chop the onion. Fry lightly in olive oil
(3) Add eggplant, zucchini, tomatoes, and basil Cook slowly for several minutes.
(4) Add 3/4 cup of wine.
(5) Stew over low heat for 20 minutes. Season with salt and pepper. Serve.

NOTE: *This is a Russian side dish.*

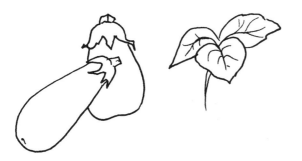

▨ INGREDIENTS

3 medium eggplants
3 medium zucchini
2 large firm tomatoes
1/2 onion
1 clove of garlic
2 tablespoons of olive oil
basil
3/4 cup of wine
salt and pepper to taste

NOTE: *This recipe came to me via an American woman who was born in China of Russian parents. I don't know if the name referred to the dish or the cook. Either way I like the swagger of the sound of Pogreonski. Gives me the impression I am at table in a dacha in a Chekhov play. Besides, the dish is a breeze to make.*

SERVES 4-6

CONCIA

(1) Trim the ends of the zucchini, and cut each one in half; slice each half thinly lengthwise. Dry on paper towels for several hours or overnight.

(2) Fry in hot olive oil until golden on both sides. Arrange in layers in a glass, porcelain, or plastic container.

(3) Season each layer with minced garlic, shredded basil leaves, salt, pepper, and a sprinkle of wine vinegar.

(4) Cover container. Store in refrigerator for several hours or a day, turning from time to time.

▨ INGREDIENTS

zucchini (See note, below)
fresh basil leaves
garlic, minced
wine vinegar salt, pepper
olive oil for frying

NOTE: *An Ancient Roman-Jewish recipe which appears in Edda Servi Machin's* The Classic Cuisine of the Italian Jews. *"Concia is practically unknown in Italy except in the Roman ghetto where it was created." In the old days the rich used it as a side dish to mixed boiled meats and the poor made a meal out of it with lots of bread. We used to love Concia between two slices of bread as a midday snack," recalled Mrs. Machlin who grew up in Tuscany. After she moved to America she served Concia as an appetizer with equal success. She gave no proportions stating that the "Piquancy of Concia depended simply on increasing or diminishing the quantity of herbs and spices."*

ZUCCHINI AND TOMATOES

(1) Slice the onions and sauté in 3 tablespoons of olive oil until translucent. Scatter over bottom of a rectangular pan, 9x12.

(2) Cut zucchini and tomatoes into uniform slices, 1/4-inch.

(3) Arrange vertically in rows, alternating one zucchini slice with one tomato slice, resulting in a striped zebra effect.

(4) Sprinkle with a teaspoon of coriander seed, 1 tablespoon of fresh thyme, salt, and pepper

(5) Spoon over all, 4 tablespoons of olive oil.

(6) Bake about 20 minutes in a fairly hot oven, 350° F. Serve.

⊞ INGREDIENTS

3 medium onions
3 tablespoons of olive oil for the onions
6 zucchini
6 Italian plum tomatoes
1 teaspoon of coriander seed
1 tablespoon of fresh thyme leaves
salt and pepper
4 tablespoons of olive oil

NOTE: A colorful and delicious preparation that seems to please everyone.

SERVES 4

ZUCCHINI WITH WALNUTS

(1) Reserve 8 walnut halves for garnish. Chop the rest.

(2) Cut the unpeeled zucchini in slices, 1/4-inch thick.

(3) Sauté in butter, gently and constantly.

(4) When almost done, add chopped walnuts, salt, and pepper.

(5) Continue cooking and stirring until zucchini is the right degree of tender.

(6) Garnish with reserved walnut halves. Serve.

▨ INGREDIENTS

1 cup of walnut halves
6 medium zucchini
2 tablespoons of butter
salt and freshly ground pepper

NOTE: *This dish has been a longtime entry in the repertory of* The Four Seasons *restaurant in* New York.

CAUTION: *Walnuts must be watched carefully because they burn easily.*

SERVES 6

DANIEL BOULUD'S SIDE DISH OF
ZUCCHINI ORANGE FLAVORED

(1) Plunge the orange zest into 1 quart of fast boiling water. Cook 2 minutes and drain.

(2) Bring a fresh quart of water to a boil. Cook the zest 5 to 7 minutes more. Strain out the zest and put aside.

(3) Heat olive oil over high heat in a large pan. Add zucchini, rosemary, salt, and pepper.

(4) Reduce heat to moderate. Cook 6 to 8 minutes. Toss to avoid coloring the zucchini. Pour on the orange juice. Cook until totally evaporated. Add zest. Test for seasoning.

(5) Arrange sliced zucchini in a bowl, zest on top. Serve warm.

▨ INGREDIENTS

1 orange (The juice plus the zest cut into a fine julienne)
2 tablespoons of olive oil
3 cups of zucchini, in 1/4-inch slices
2 tablespoons of rosemary, chopped
salt and freshly ground pepper

NOTE: A sunny accompaniment to broiled fish or chicken.

SERVES 4

MILD VEGETABLE CURRY

(1) Heat the curry powder in oil. Stir. Pay attention. Curry powder can burn. Add onions and cook for 1 minute over medium heat.

(2) Add broth. Add potato. Cook 5 minutes.

(3) Add carrots. Cook 5 minutes.

(4) Add zucchini. Cook 5 minutes.

(5) Add yogurt and mint just long enough to warm through. (If heated too long, the yogurt will break down.)

⬛ INGREDIENTS

2 tablespoons of olive oil
1 tablespoon of curry powder
2 medium onions, quartered
2 cups of chicken broth
2 medium potatoes, cut into
   3/4-inch cubes
3/4 pound of carrots, cut into
   3/4-inch cubes
1 pound of zucchini, cut into
   slices 3/4-inches thick
1 cup of natural yogurt
mint
salt

NOTE: Each vegetable retains its form and distinction. The overall is pleasantly different.

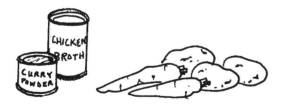

SERVES 4-6

ZUCCHINI AND CHERRY
TOMATO SALAD

(1) Wash salad leaves. Dry completely
As everyone knows, any trace of
water in a salad is a big No No.
(2) Rub salad bowl with a cut clove of
garlic.
(3) Mix zucchini, cherry tomatoes,
parsley, basil, and salad leaves with
a good vinaigrette. Serve.

▧ INGREDIENTS

2 or 3 varieties of salad leaves.
Romaine, Bibb, Boston,
Arugola, leaf lettuce... torn by
hand
2 small zucchini, cut in matchsticks
12 cherry tomatoes. cut in half
basil and flat parsley

A GOOD VINAIGRETTE
salt and pepper
2 parts of wine vinegar
5 parts of olive oil
Mix well and that is all there is
to it.

SERVES 4

ZUCCHINI AND HEARTS OF PALM

(1) Split the hearts-of-palm length-wise.
(2) Arrange 4 in a row on individual salad plates. A lettuce leaf at one end.
(3) Cut zucchini into thin cross slices. Arrange between the heart-of-palm halves.
(4) Dress with a good French vinai-grette.

NOTE: Simple tropical splendor.

INGREDIENTS

12 hearts-of-palm
1 zucchini
6 bibb lettuce leaves
vinaigrette (see page 76)

NOTE: A classic from the Four Seasons Restaurant in New York. The delicate hearts-of-palm are available in tins from Brazil and Florida The source is the Sabal palmetto. They are particularly good in salads.

SERVES 6

PEAR AND ZUCCHINI SALAD

(1) Cut zucchini into matchsticks.

(2) Peel and cube the pears.

(3) Shave Parmesan into thin leaves.

(4) Make a bed of arugula on each plate.

(5) Top with zucchini match-sticks and pear cubes. Cover with 3 to 4 Parmesan leaves per person.

(6) Spoon lemon vinaigrette over each salad.

For the Vinaigrette

(1) Dissolve 1 teaspoon of salt and freshly ground pepper in 2 tablespoons of lemon juice.

(2) Add 5 to 6 tablespoons of good olive oil. Mix well. Serve.

NOTE: *An inspired combination.*

◈ INGREDIENTS

4 small zucchini or 3 medium

2 pears, ripe but firm

12 to 16 shaved leaves of fresh Parmesan

Arugula, enough to make a bed of greens on four individual salad plates

Lemon Vinaigrette
salt
pepper
lemon juice
olive oil

NOTE: *We first tasted this pleasurable starter at Angeletti, a small restaurant on the Piazza Angeletti in Rome.*

SERVES 4

TOO HOT TO COOK–ALMOST TOO HOT TO EAT
SALAD FOR A MID-SUMMER'S DAY

(1) Choose a cool salad bowl of glass or porcelain.

(2) Peel a lemon and cut in quarters. Squeeze a lemon. Place lemon juice and lemon quarters in bowl.

(3) Add the zucchini, the tomato cubes, and a sprinkle of sea salt.

(4) Add olives and a handful of fresh herbs. Give a twist of the pepper mill. Pour on the very best virgin olive oil.

Set a table under a shady tree.

▩ INGREDIENTS

2 lemons

3 small zucchini, cut crosswise into 1/8-inch slices

2 medium tomatoes, diced

8 pitted black olives

fresh herbs: mint, coriander, or basil and flat parsley

season with sea salt, olive oil, and freshly ground pepper

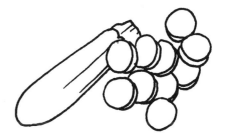

SERVES 2-3

ZUCCHINI WHISKY CAKE

(1) Soak raisins in whisky. Set aside for 15 minutes or more.
(2) Beat sugar and eggs. Add the peanut oil.
(3) Sift in gradually.... flour, baking powder, baking soda, salt, and cinnamon.
(4) Add shredded zucchini, grated lemon zest, walnuts, raisins and the whisky not already absorbed by the raisins.
(5) Pour into loaf pans or a 10-inch round cake pan.

Preheat the oven to 350° F.

(6) Bake for 30 to 35 minutes. Test for doneness.
(7) Cool for 10 minutes before turning out onto a wire rack. Spread the Cream Cheese Topping over the top.

⬛ INGREDIENTS

1/2 cup of raisins
1 1/3 cup of whisky (approx.)
1 cup of sugar
2 large eggs
1/2 cup of peanut oil
2 1/2 cups of flour
2 teaspoons of baking powder
1 teaspoon of baking soda
1/2 teaspoon of salt
1/2 teaspoon of cinnamon
2 cups of coarsely grated zucchini
grated zest of 1 large lemon
1 cup of chopped walnuts

CREAM CHEESE TOPPING

4 ounces of cream cheese
1 cup of confectioners' sugar
juice of 1 lemon
grated zest of 1 lemon

(1) Mash the cream cheese.
(2) Blend with lemon juice, lemon zest, and confectioners' sugar.

COOKIE BARS

(1) Grate zucchini. Discard any liquid they may run off.
(2) Cream butter and the two sugars.
(3) Beat in the eggs.
(4) Sift in flour, baking powder, and salt. Mix well.
(5) Stir in chopped nuts, soaked raisins, and shredded coconut.
(6) Turn into 2 buttered and floured 8x10-inch pans.

Preheat the oven to 350° F.

(7) Place the pans in the oven and bake until cookie tester comes out clean. About 30 minutes. Score into rectangular bars.
(8) Cool in pans for 10 minutes before inverting onto racks to cool completely.
(9) Spread with mascarpone sweetened to taste.

▧ INGREDIENTS

2 cups of zucchini, shredded
3/4 cup of butter, softened
1/2 cup of white sugar
1/2 cup of brown sugar
2 eggs
1 and 3/4 cups of flour
1 1/2 teaspoons of baking powder
1/4 teaspoon of salt
1 cup of walnuts, coarsely chopped
1/2 cup of raisins, soaked in rum, Cognac or whisky for 20 minutes
1 cup of shredded coconut
mascarpone sweetened to taste

NOTE: *These delectable cookie bars are moist. Liners will keep them from sticking to the pans.*

GRATIN OF ZUCCHINI

(1) Place zucchini and butter in sauce pan. Cover and cook over slow fire until zucchini has given up its water. About 12 minutes. Lift lid and stir from time to time.

(2) Remove from heat and transfer zucchini to a large bowl. Mix with the cream and half the grated cheese. Add diced ham. Season with salt, pepper, cayenne, and chopped parsley.

(3) Turn into a gratin dish. Sprinkle surface with the remaining Gruyère.

(4) Bake in a moderately hot oven 15 to 20 minutes until golden brown.

NOTE: *Easy, Easy. Super Satisfying.*

▣ INGREDIENTS

2 pounds of zucchini, sliced
2 ounces of butter
3/4 cup of heavy cream
1/2 pound of grated Gruyère cheese, half reserved
1 thickly sliced cooked ham, cut into large diced chunks
a pinch of salt and pepper
cayenne
chopped flat parsley

NOTE: *Supposedly for 4, but two of us demolish it with pleasure.*

SERVES 4

ZUCCHINI DRESSED UP
IN A WRAPPER OF HAM

(1) Trim ends of the zucchini. Steam approximately 15 minutes. Slice lengthwise without severing the 2 halves.

(2) Sauté mushrooms and garlic in butter. Season with salt and pepper. Spread mushroom mixture sandwich fashion between the 2 halves. Close and wrap each filled zucchini in its slice of ham.

(3) Line up the ham rolls in a baking dish, seam side down. Cover with a Cheese Béchamel. Sprinkle surface with grated Parmesan.

(4) Bake in hot oven until sauce is bubbly and golden brown. Dust with chopped parsley before serving.

CHEESE BÉCHAMEL

(1) Melt the butter over low heat.

(2) Incorporate the flour.

(3) Little by little add the milk, stirring constantly to avoid lumps as the mixture thickens.

(4) Add cheese. Continue to stir until melted. Season with salt, pepper, and grated nutmeg.

✦ INGREDIENTS

2 small zucchini per person
6-8 mushrooms, chopped fine
1 large clove garlic, minced
butter for sauté
salt and pepper
ham, one thin slice for each zucchini large enough for a complete wraparound
Cheese Béchamel
Parmesan cheese, grated
chopped flat parsley

CHEESE BÉCHAMEL

2 tablespoons of butter
2 tablespoons of flour
1 cup of warm milk
4 ounces of Gruyère cheese, grated
salt and pepper
nutmeg, grated

NOTE: Count 2 ham rolls per person. Multiply ingredients according to number of persons to be served.

USEFUL AS A TRICK UP YOUR SLEEVE

(1) Slice zucchini crosswise, 1/8-inch thick.
(2) Melt 2 tablespoons of butter in a large saucepan. Add zucchini and 1 teaspoon of salt.
(3) Cook over medium-high heat, stirring until all the water has evaporated from the zucchini.
(4) Add 2 crushed cloves of garlic, 1 teaspoon of thyme and cook 2 minutes more.
(5) Remove from heat. Add 2 tablespoons of olive oil. Mix well. Check seasoning.
(6) Should be eaten tepid.

NOTE: Holds up well for next day eating.

▨ INGREDIENTS

2 pounds of small zucchini
2 tablespoons of butter
1 teaspoon of salt
2 cloves of garlic
1 teaspoon of thyme
2 tablespoons of olive oil

ZUCCHINI ALA SCAPECE

(1) Fry zucchini in olive oil until golden brown. This may be done in several batches. Drain well on absorbent paper.

(2) Place a layer of zucchini on a large flat plate or rimmed dish. Sprinkle with mint, garlic, cinnamon sugar, salt, and pepper. Repeat layers until you have used all the zucchini. Pour over the vinegar. Leave to marinate several hours or overnight. Serve.

NOTE: All "Sweet and Sour" did not originate in China. This preparation is a long time specialty of Naples.

✥ INGREDIENTS

6-8 small, firm zucchini, thinly sliced and patted dry
olive oil
1/3 cup of fresh mint leaves torn into pieces
2 cloves of garlic, minced
pinch of cinnamon sugar
salt to taste
freshly ground pepper
2 tablespoons of mild wine vinegar
2 tablespoons of sugar

ZUCCHINI CUPS
FILLED WITH MUSHROOMS

(1) Trim the zucchini and cut each one cross-wise into 4 equal parts.

(2) Hollow sections. You will now have 16 upright cups. The walls of the cups should be 3 1/8-inches thick.

(3) Dissolve 1 bouillon cube in 1 cup of hot water.

(4) Stand the cups in a baking dish. Place a little butter in the bottom of each cup.

(5) Fill the cavities with hot bouillon. Pour the remaining bouillon into the bottom of the dish. Cover with aluminum foil. Bake in a moderate oven for 17 minutes. Drain cups by turning upside down.

(6) Transfer bouillon into a small saucepan. Reduce to 2 tablespoons. Paint the inside and outside of cups with the reduced bouillon.

(7) While the zucchini cups are baking in the oven, prepare the mushroom filling. Heat a little butter and olive oil in a sauce pan. When sizzling–but not burnt–add the minced shallot and the minced mushrooms. Cook briskly until mushrooms give up their water. Remove from heat.

(8) Mix with the heavy cream and finely chopped parsley. Season with pepper. Fill the cups. Sprinkle tops with parsley. Serve.

NOTE: A low cost, high profile starter.

NOTE: *Arrange 4 cups on each of 4 plates. Although this is meant to be a starter, 4 of these delicious zucchini cups could be the basis of a light lunch.*

▨ INGREDIENTS

4 zucchini, 5-6 inches long
1 bouillon cube
butter
olive oil
4 medium mushrooms, minced
1 small shallot, minced
salt and pepper
2 tablespoons of crème fraîche
    or heavy cream
chopped parsley

SERVES 4

SPAGHETTI PRIMAVERA

(1) Cook peas in boiling, salted water for 3 minutes. Drain and hold aside.

(2) Cook broccoli flowerets in boiling, salted water for 3 minutes. Refresh under cold water to stop the cooking. Drain and hold aside.

(3) Cook asparagus tips in boiling salted water. 5 minutes. Drain and hold aside.

(4) Toast pine nuts in a dry non-stick pan for 45 seconds. Keep shaking pan so pine nuts do not burn. Hold aside.

(5) Warm 3 tablespoons of olive oil with a clove of smashed garlic. Remove garlic after 30 seconds by which time it will have imparted its flavor to the oil. Add leeks and sauté 5 minutes. Add zucchini and mushrooms. Cook 5 minutes.

(6) Add tomatoes. Cook 2 minutes.

(7) Add the pre-cooked peas, broccoli, and asparagus tips. Mix all vegetables together and keep warm. Stir in the toasted pine nuts.

(8) Boil spaghetti in a large quantity of salted water. 1 tablespoon of olive oil in the water will keep the spaghetti from sticking together. Cook until al dente. Drain and return to pot.

(9) Add a lump of butter, 1/4 cup of grated Parmesan and the mixed vegetables. Sprinkle with chopped parsley Turn all around in the heated pot. Serve with side bowl of grated Parmesan and basil.

OPTIONAL: Sirio Maccione, owner of Le Cirque, the famous Manhattan restaurant, adds the following flourish to his version of *Spaghetti Primavera*... Stir 3 tablespoons of butter, 3/4 cup heavy cream, 3 tablespoons of mascarpone and 1/4 cup grated Parmesan over low heat. Season with salt and pepper. Mix together with vegetable mixture and pasta.

NOTE: The recipe may seem complicat-
ed, but it is mainly a question of
organization and assembly, although
for a few minutes, hands have to
move on the double quick. The result
however, is suave and exquisite.

There is no cut and dried recipe
for this spring-time pasta. Add new
green peas and fresh baby limas if
you are lucky to have them.

Other possible entries: diced bell peppers, leaves of spinach or arugula,
sliced radishes, quartered artichoke
hearts.

▣ INGREDIENTS

peas
1 1/2 cups of broccoli flowerets
10-12 asparagus tips, cut into 1
  inch lengths
2 tablespoons of toasted pine nuts
3 tablespoons of olive oil
1 garlic clove, crushed
1 leek, thinly sliced, white part
  only
4 small zucchini, diced
1 cup of sliced mushrooms
  (Shiitake, if you can)
2 plum tomatoes, seeded and
  diced
1 pound of spaghetti
butter
Parmesan cheese, grated (1/4 cup
  for pasta and more reserved as
  topping)
flat parsley
fresh basil
salt and pepper

INDEX

Traditional Country Life Recipe Books from
BRICK TOWER PRESS

For sales, editorial information, subsidiary rights information or a catalog, please write or phone or e-mail to

Brick Tower Press
1230 Park Avenue
New York, NY 10128, US
Sales: 1-800-68-BRICK
Tel: 212-427-7139 Fax: 212-860-8852
www.BrickTowerPress.com • bookmanuscript.com
email: bricktower@aol.com.

For Canadian sales please contact our distributor,
Vanwell Publishing Ltd.
1 Northrup Crescent, Box 2131
St. Catharines, ON L2R 7S2
Tel: 905-937-3100

For sales in the UK and Europe please contact our distributor,
Gazelle Book Services
Falcon House, Queens Square
Lancaster, LA1 1RN, UK
Tel: (01524) 68765 Fax: (01524) 63232
email: gazelle4go@aol.com.

For Australian and New Zealand sales please contact
INT Press Distribution Pyt. Ltd.
386 Mt. Alexander Road
Ascot Vale, VIC 3032, Australia
Tel: 61-3-9326 2416 Fax: 61-3-9326 2413
email: sales@intpress.com.au.

Forthcoming titles:

Pie Companion
Ice Creams
Bakery Companion
Salmon Companion
Honey

MAIL ORDER AND GENERAL INFORMATION

Many of our titles are carried by your local book store or gift and museum shop. If they do not already carry our line please ask them to write us for information.

If you are unable to purchase our titles from your local shop, call or write to us. Our titles are available through mail order. Just send us a check or money order for $9.95 per title with $1.50 postage (shipping is free with 3 or more assorted copies) to the address below or call us Monday through Friday, 9 AM to 5PM, EST. We accept Visa, Mastercard, and American Express cards.

Other titles in this series:

American Chef's Companion
Chocolate Companion
Fresh Herb Companion
Thanksgiving Cookery
Victorian Christmas Cookery
Apple Companion
Pumpkin Companion
Soups, Stews & Chowders
Fresh Bread Companion
Sandwich Companion
Farmstand-Vegetables
Cranberry Companion